Muffins

FAST AND FANTASTIC

THIRD EDITION

SUSAN REIMER

CHERRY TREE PUBLICATIONS
EDINBURGH

Muffins
FAST AND FANTASTIC

Published by Cherry Tree Publications
P.O. Box 28606
Edinburgh EH14 5ZH

Photography by Richard Mountney, design by Charles Barr

First published in Great Britain 1996
Second edition, revised and enlarged 1999
Reprinted 1996, 1997 (four times), 1998 (four times),
1999 (three times), 2000 (three times)
Third edition, revised and enlarged June 2001
Reprinted November 2001, 2002 (twice)

British Library Cataloguing in Publication Data
Data available

ISBN 0 9528858 2 4

(2nd edition: ISBN 0 9528858 1 6)
(1st edition: ISBN 0 9528858 0 8)

Printed in Great Britain by Oxuniprint
at Oxford University Press, Great Clarendon Street,
Oxford OX2 6DP

CONTENTS

Introduction 5
Notes on Muffin-Making 7
Basic Muffin 12
Apple Spice 14
Apricot Almond 16
Banana 16
Banana Oatmeal 16
Blueberry (see Summer Fruit) 58
Bran 18
Bran Cinnamon 18
Buttermilk 20
Butterscotch Raisin 20
Carrot 22
Carrot Bran 22
Carrot Pineapple 24
Cheddar Bran 18
Cheese 56
Cherry Walnut 24
Chocolate 26
Chocolate Cheesecake 26
Chocolate Cherry 26
Chocolate Chip 12
Chocolate Hazelnut 26
Chocolate Iced 26
Chocolate Mocha 26
Chocolate Orange 26
Cinnamon Crunch 28
Cocoa Courgette 30
Coffee Date-Walnut 32
Cornmeal 30
Cranberry 32
Date Walnut 32
Double Chocolate 26
Gingerbread 34
Gluten-Free 60
Lemon 36
Lemon Poppy Seed 36
Lemon Raisin 36
Maple Pecan 38
Marmalade Apricot 40
Mincemeat Sultana 40
Oatmeal Chocolate Chip (or Fruit) 42
Oatmeal Yogurt 44
Orange 48
Orange-Carrot Spice 46
Orange-Date Bran 50
Orange Poppy Seed 48
Peach 50
Pear Ginger 52
Pineapple 52
Poppy Seed 54
Pumpkin 54
Rhubarb 50
Savoury Cheese 56
Summer Fruit 58
Tropical Fruit 58
Appendix 1: Gluten-Free and Wheat-Free Baking 60
      Gluten-Free Banana 61
      Gluten-Free Apple Spice 62
Appendix 2: North American Measures and Equivalents 64

ACKNOWLEDGMENTS

Even a small book can incur many debts of gratitude:
I owe my greatest thanks to my husband, David, for believing in this "little project" and giving his indefatigable support.

To Richard and Charlie, thank you for making a dream come true!

Useful feedback was provided by the Centre for Nutrition and Food Research at Queen Margaret College in Edinburgh, and the Department of Diabetes at the Royal Infirmary in Edinburgh.

Rombauer and Becker's *Joy of Cooking* was an invaluable source of information which almost always had answers to my questions.

I greatly appreciate the bountiful enthusiasm and helpful comments given by family and friends. This book would not be the same without them.

Special thanks to my Mum for teaching me the joys of fresh baking and much more. Your baking was the inspiration for many of these recipes.

To David, Lydia and Philip
Who, having tested millions of muffins, are happy to eat millions more.

INTRODUCTION

"What do you call these? Are they cakes? buns? cookies?" When I first published *Muffins* in 1996, muffins were largely unknown in Britain. Now, with the recent explosion of interest in international foods, I am happy to say that those perplexed responses to my Canadian baking are quite rare. In fact, *Muffins* has received an overwhelmingly positive response and as a result has gone through successive editions. For many people, *Muffins* has not only prompted their first attempts at home-baking, but has provided their first successes as well.

Among the enhancements in this third edition, I am pleased to include recipes and tips for delicious gluten-free and wheat-free muffins; this spells the end to dense powdery odd-tasting baking! The information provided will also be helpful for adapting your own recipes to suit gluten- and wheat-free diets.

The muffins in this book are simple to make and quick to bake, as well as being nutritious. This makes them a great alternative to junk food! Crisps and chocolate bars, which dominate today's snack scene, offer little nutritional value: crisps are high in both fat and salt while chocolate bars are high in fat and sugar. Home-made muffins, on the other hand, offer a good balance of carbohydrate, protein and fat. Many of them contain the added goodness of fruits, vegetables, nuts, oats and bran. Muffins are economical to make and offer a wide variety of delicious options: some are traditionally eaten at breakfast, but all are suitable for snacks and tea-time. With flavours covering the whole spectrum of sweet to savoury, there is plenty of choice here for everyone!

The history of the North American muffin is elusive. The flat yeast-leavened "English" muffin bears no resemblance to the peaked cake-like "American" muffin which uses baking powder as its raising agent.

The latter type of muffin can be found in late 19th century American cookery books but its origins and development are difficult to trace. With recipes early travelling north into Canada, the muffin was soon shared between those two cultures. Over the past few decades, muffin popularity has grown to such an extent that they can be commonly found right across Canada and the United States. Muffins are still changing and developing today: trans-Atlantic visitors may have encountered the recent fashion for "mega muffins" and "muffin tops"! Whatever happens with these fads, they bear witness to the infinite adaptability of the muffin.

Muffins were an integral part of my Canadian lifestyle. Baking them each week to enjoy fresh, as well as to stock the freezer for snacks and lunch-boxes, was a basic part of family routine. This came under threat when I first moved to Britain. Anyone who has had opportunity to cook in both Britain and North America will know that some recipes cannot be simply transferred from one country to another. Frustration grows as favourite recipes fail, time after time, for no apparent reason. Eventually my love of baking spurred me on to find the answer.

Two main problems emerged: flour and measurement. The difference in flour accounts for the majority of "flops". You can read more about this under "Notes on Muffin-Making". Likewise the difference in measurement creates no end of trouble. For instance, many people do not realize that a "cup" in North America is a standard measure of 8 fluid ounces (240 ml), whereas a "cup" in Britain can apparently range from 6-10 fluid ounces depending on the size of one's teacup!

Compounding this problem, there is also confusion over the word "ounce". In Canada and the United States, "ounce" is assumed to mean "fluid ounce", as North Americans are accustomed to measuring all ingredients by volume. Indeed, my standard Canadian measuring jug which indicates "ounces" on its side is actually measuring "fluid ounces"; this use of the word "ounce" in North America must not be confused with weight measure. On page 64, I have included approximate volume equivalents for the weights used in this book.

Once the mystery had been unravelled, I began to make muffins again in earnest and was delighted by the interest and enthusiasm shown by friends here. Thus inspired, I set to work developing muffin recipes for the British kitchen, keeping two criteria firmly in mind: they must be healthy *and* tasty. Over the years, I have encountered many muffin recipes that are no different from cake, and also recipes that try to be so healthy as to be almost inedible! With my background in health sciences, naturally I am keen to promote healthy eating. But with two hungry teenagers, I also know the importance of making food that tastes good! By using low to moderate amounts of sugar and fat, I have tried to achieve a well-balanced muffin.

Every one of these muffins is a favourite in our home and has been tested many, many times. My aim is to give you a delicious and successful introduction to the world of muffins. For most, the variety offered in this book will be more than sufficient for a lifetime of muffin-baking. And for those who have an insatiable appetite for new and different flavours, this book will give the confidence and know-how to develop those individual muffin creations!

The technique for making muffins is simple, but quite different from other forms of baking. So please read the following notes on muffin-making before you begin – following them can make the difference between success and failure! Paragraphs marked by ➤ offer advice for special diets.

Sift together dry ingredients.

Stir together wet ingredients.

Pour wet mixture into dry and stir just to combine. Spoon lumpy batter into muffin tins.

NOTES ON MUFFIN-MAKING

MEASURING AND MIXING

Standardized measuring spoons and jug are essential for successful baking. All measurements with the spoons are level unless stated otherwise. Measurements in the jug should be made at eye-level for accuracy.

Muffin mixing is very quick and simple. In fact, the key to successful muffins is to keep the mixing as brief as possible once the wet and dry ingredients are combined. Generally the dry ingredients are sifted together in one bowl, and the wet ingredients are stirred together in a separate bowl. (The dry ingredients can be prepared in advance but wet and dry must not be combined until just before baking, as liquid will activate the raising agent.) The wet mixture is then poured all at one time into the dry and the two are stirred – not beaten – just until combined. This final mixing must be with a spoon, never a whisk or electric mixer. It should take only about 30 seconds, just until the batter appears evenly mixed but still lumpy. No dry flour should be visible. (I prefer to use a metal dessert spoon for stirring as it is more effective than a wooden spoon for scraping the bottom and sides of the bowl during mixing.) Muffin batter should not pour ribbon-like off the spoon, but rather should drop in loose globs.

Over-stirring has a detrimental effect on the flour which will result in a disappointing muffin. With British plain flour, over-stirring breaks down the delicate gluten, producing a dense texture. In North America, all-purpose flour contains a tougher gluten which produces a coarse texture when over-stirred.

INGREDIENTS

Flour – plain flour, produced from soft wheat, contains a delicate form of gluten which makes it ideal for muffin-making (as with cakes and pastry). Strong flour (for bread-making) on the other hand, is made from hard wheat which contains much more and tougher gluten; this produces an elasticity suitable for yeast-leavened breads but not muffins.

Self-raising flour is an acceptable alternative to plain flour. If this is your flour of choice, note the alterations given for the amount of baking powder required. Do not omit bicarbonate of soda when it is called for. Two notes here: one drawback of self-raising flour is that it is difficult to ensure the raising agent is fresh, especially if you do not bake regularly. Second, self-raising flour in North America usually contains salt; in this case you should omit the salt called for in the recipe. In Britain, self-raising flour does not contain salt.

Wholemeal flour can be used in place of white flour. However I would recommend a half-and-half combination to maintain a light texture. For those who are less keen on wholemeal flour, even substituting a small amount, say 1-2 oz (30-60 g), will increase the fibre and nutritional content.

Two further important points about flour. First, sifting the flour together with the raising agent and salt will ensure an even distribution and minimize lumps. Second, be prepared to adjust the amount of liquid if you are finding the batter too thick or thin. Flour varies in its ability to absorb moisture depending on the type of wheat, processing and storage. Also, after experimenting with several brands of plain flour, I was surprised to find that they produced different volumes for the same weight! All of this made it difficult to give precise liquid measurements. Just bear in mind that most muffin batters should drop off the spoon in loose globs.

In Canada and the United States, all-purpose flour (a blend of soft and hard wheat) is normally used for muffins and breads. When baking in North America, refer to the approximate volume equivalents given on page 64 which can only be a rough guide due to the numerous variables involved. Note that less all-purpose flour is needed than plain flour.

Gluten-free and wheat-free flours are discussed in Appendix 1 (page 60).

Baking powder and *bicarbonate of soda* are not interchangeable. A quick science lesson here: baking powder contains both an acid and an alkaline substance which react with each other in the presence of moisture to form a gas; this creates tiny bubbles which expand the batter. Bicarbonate of soda, on the other hand, is solely alkaline; it can only help the leavening process if it is used in combination with an acid ingredient such as buttermilk. Some acidic ingredients such as chocolate or honey are not strong enough to be the only source of acid, so certain recipes call for both baking powder and bicarbonate of soda. The small amount of bicarbonate of soda neutralizes the acid ingredients while the main leavening action is left to the baking powder. (Be sure your raising agents are fresh, as their effectiveness deteriorates with time, especially when exposed to air. If they were opened several months ago, throw them out!)

Salt is used primarily to enhance flavour but it also affects texture. It can be reduced if necessary but should not be omitted.

Sugar is used both for flavour and texture. Remember that the sugar content of muffins can be adjusted either up or down to suit individual tastes. I have indicated this in a few of the recipes but the same can be done for all. Fine white granulated sugar (such as caster sugar) and soft brown sugars are best as they are easily absorbed into the baked goods. (White sugar can be mixed with either the wet or dry ingredients, but soft brown sugar distributes better if added to the wet ingredients.) Regular white granulated sugar is usually fine enough to give a good result, but unrefined sugars such as "golden granulated" and "demerara" will remain gritty in the final product.

➤ *In the diabetic diet it is necessary to restrict sugar intake. A very small amount of sugar in baking is considered acceptable when this is part of an overall healthy diet. The sugar in each of the recipes should be reduced to 2 Tablespoons (30 ml) or less, and sweet toppings, syrups and chocolate should be omitted. It is also important to increase fibre and decrease fat consumed in the diabetic diet. Hence the following recommendations: use a combination of wholemeal and white flour, use reduced fat milk, use vegetable oil rather than butter, and use slightly less oil than stated. Add a little extra liquid to compensate. As the lower sugar and fat content will have an effect on texture, always serve the muffins warm to make this less noticeable.*

Honey is useful not only for its sweetening quality but also its subtle flavour and golden brown colour in baking. When its natural acidity reacts with bicarbonate of soda it can also boost the rising process.

Molasses and **black treacle** can be used interchangeably for the recipes in this book. This is only possible because the stated quantities are small; it does not mean they are the same. Molasses is available in three forms: light table molasses (commonly used in North America), dark molasses, and bitter blackstrap molasses. Black treacle is a blend of dark molasses and other syrups. Take note: when using North American recipes that call for table molasses, substituting black treacle will give disappointing results. Adjustments must be made for black treacle's strong flavour and less acidic properties.

Eggs enhance the texture, rising and nutritional value of baked foods. These recipes are based on medium (size 3 and 4) eggs but other sizes should not be a problem for single batches.

➤ *For those who cannot include eggs in their diet, omit the egg and increase the amount of liquid by 3-4 Tablespoons (45-60 ml). If only the yolk needs to be omitted, substitute 1 or 2 egg whites instead.*

Milk – semi-skimmed, skimmed and whole milk all work equally well. Powdered milk is a very economical alternative to fresh milk, with no noticeable difference in flavour when used in baking. Please note that when buttermilk is called for (see page 20), bicarbonate of soda must be used as the raising agent in order to produce a good flavour and texture.

➤ *For those who cannot include milk in their diet, use milk substitutes, fruit juice or water instead. The muffins will not rise quite as high but it is unlikely anyone will notice!*

Oil – I have specified vegetable oil as it has a mild flavour suitable for baking and usually contains a high proportion of rapeseed oil. Rapeseed oil (also known as canola oil) has become popular recently due to its low saturated fat content and other health benefits. Olive oil is not recommended for baking because of its strong flavour.

➤ *Although I have indicated a choice of vegetable oil or butter for most of the recipes, dieticians recommend vegetable oil as the healthier option as it is significantly lower in saturated fat. I also find it more economical and easier to use than butter. However, some people prefer the richer flavour of butter. As a compromise, you might like to use a combination of the two. In some recipes soft butter (or margarine) is needed for the method of mixing.*

For those who prefer to cut back on the fat content, the quantity can be reduced by 1 fluid ounce (30 ml) vegetable oil or 1 ounce (30 g) butter. The muffins will not be as tender as a result but this can be made less noticeable by serving warm. I do not recommend cutting back any further than this as the texture becomes chewy rather than tender.

Butter – where butter is called for, a suitable margarine can also be used. (Check the label.) For health reasons, avoid hard margarines: these contain transfatty acids which apparently do us more harm than saturated fat. (Note: hot melted butter must not be added directly to the beaten egg as it would cook the egg instantly. Always cool the butter slightly and add ingredients in the order given.)

Wheatgerm forms the most nutritious part of the wheat kernel, and is a natural source of folic acid, vitamin E, thiamine and iron. It has a mild nutty flavour, and should be stored in the refrigerator. A spoonful of wheatgerm can be added to all your baking for extra nutrition.

Fruit – dried fruit tends to absorb moisture from the batter, whereas fresh fruit and vegetables release juice into the batter during baking. This should be kept in mind when adapting or creating muffin recipes.

BAKING

For best results use proper muffin tins of either standard or mini-size. A standard muffin cup is about 3 cm deep and 7 cm in diameter across the top. Mini-muffins are fun for parties and smaller appetites. The recipes in this book will produce 10-12 standard-size muffins or approximately 36 mini-muffins (or 6 standard plus 12 mini!). Extra-large ("Texas-style") tins will enable you to make 5 or 6 jumbo muffins.

Shallow bun tins are not recommended, as the muffins cannot achieve their correct shape and height. However, if this is all that is available, decrease baking time to about 15 minutes.

Prepare your muffin tins either by lining with paper cases or by greasing with a solid vegetable fat or margarine. Oil sprays are also available in most supermarkets. If using grease, allow muffins to cool for several minutes to make removal easier. Cooling also helps paper cases peel off more easily.

Ideally, muffins have a raised symmetrical top although the actual height will depend on the contents of the batter and how much is put into each muffin cup. Several factors can prevent a muffin from rising properly: low oven temperature, stale raising agent, overly thick batter (muffins are hard and small) or thin batter (muffins spread out over the pan instead of up). Very pointy or distorted tops indicate the oven temperature is too hot or uneven.

Muffins should be baked in a moderately hot, preheated oven, so 375-400°F (190-200°C) in a conventional oven. For fan ovens, the temperature should be lowered to approximately 170°C (refer to the manufacturer's instructions). With a gas oven, use Gas Mark 5-6 if baking on the middle rack, or Gas Mark 4-5 if baking nearer the top of the oven. Ovens vary in their temperature distribution and accuracy so you will need to discover what works best with yours.

Standard-size muffins should take about 20-25 minutes to bake in a conventional or gas oven, mini-muffins about 15 minutes and jumbo muffins about 30-35 minutes. Muffins are done when the tops are lightly browned and spring back (or feel quite firm) when pressed gently. If your finger leaves an indent, continue baking for another 2-3 minutes and test again. (For jumbo muffins, it is best to test with a metal cake-tester as the top can become brown before the inside is fully cooked.) If the muffins require either more or less time than stated above, make appropriate adjustments to your oven temperature for future batches.

STORING AND FREEZING

Muffins are at their best when freshly baked and still warm. Ideally, any not eaten on the day of baking should be frozen as soon as possible to maintain freshness. Muffins freeze very well. Simply cool them to room temperature and freeze in airtight bags or containers – perfect for taking out whenever needed, and in just the right quantity! If freezing is not possible, store muffins in an airtight container and eat within two days. Warm before serving to restore freshness.

A frozen muffin, wrapped in a lunch box first thing in the morning, will be thawed by lunch-time. For instant thawing, microwave unwrapped at Medium for 30-40 seconds. With a conventional oven, heat frozen muffins for 10-15 minutes at 350°F (175°C), unwrapped for a crusty muffin, wrapped in foil for a soft one.

THE BASIC MUFFIN

Delicious even in its simplest state, this muffin invites creative variation! For a basic buttermilk version, see page 20.

Makes 9-11 standard-size

9 oz (255 g) plain flour*
3 teaspoons (15 ml) baking powder
$1/2$ teaspoon (2.5 ml) salt
3-4 oz (85-110 g) fine white granulated sugar
1 egg
8 fl oz (240 ml) milk
3 fl oz (90 ml) vegetable oil or 3 oz (85 g) butter, melted

With self-raising flour, decrease baking powder to 1 teaspoon (5 ml).

Method

1 Prepare muffin tins with liners or grease. Preheat oven to 375-400°F (190-200°C) for a conventional oven, Gas Mark 5-6. (See page 10 for fan ovens and further guidelines.)
2 In a large bowl, sift together: flour, baking powder, salt and sugar.
3 In a separate bowl, beat egg with a fork. Stir in milk, followed by oil/melted butter.
4 Pour all of liquid ingredients into the dry mixture. Stir just until combined, scraping sides and bottom of the bowl as you stir. This mixing should take only about 30 seconds. The batter will be lumpy but no dry flour should be visible. Do not over-stir.
5 Fill muffin cups three-quarters full. Bake for 20-25 minutes until tops are lightly browned and spring back when pressed gently. Allow muffins to cool for several minutes to make removal easier. Best served warm.

Chocolate Chip Muffins
Add 3 oz (85 g) plain chocolate chips to the dry ingredients. Add 1 teaspoon (5 ml) vanilla essence/flavouring to the wet ingredients, if desired.

Nutty Chocolate Chip Muffins
Same as chocolate chip muffins with the addition of 3 oz (85 g) of your favourite nuts, chopped.

Dried Fruit Muffins
Many interesting varieties of dried fruit are now available such as mango and pineapple. You don't have to limit yourself to raisins! Use 3-5 oz (85-140 g) chopped dried fruit to suit your taste. You might need to increase the liquid by 1-2 Tablespoons (15-30 ml) to allow for moisture being absorbed by the dried fruit.

APPLE SPICE MUFFINS

Always a popular flavour! Adjust the spices to suit your taste. Mixed spice (not to be confused with allspice) is a lovely blend of sweet spices including cinnamon, coriander seed, caraway seed, nutmeg, ginger and cloves.

Makes 10-12 standard-size

9 oz (255 g) plain flour*

3 teaspoons (15 ml) baking powder

1/2 teaspoon (2.5 ml) salt

1 1/2 teaspoons (7.5 ml) mixed spice (or try 1 1/2 teaspoons cinnamon plus 1/4 teaspoon nutmeg and a pinch of ginger and cloves)

3-4 oz (85-110 g) fine white granulated sugar

1 egg

6 oz (170 g) finely chopped apple (I like to use Granny Smiths, but most other types should work just as well)

5 fl oz (150 ml) milk

3 fl oz (90 ml) vegetable oil or 3 oz (85 g) butter, melted

2-3 oz (60-85 g) raisins, sultanas or chopped walnuts (optional)

Optional Topping:

3 Tablespoons (45 ml) soft brown sugar

2 oz (60 g) walnuts, chopped

*With self-raising flour, reduce baking powder to 1 teaspoon (5 ml).

Method

1 Prepare muffin tins. Preheat oven to 375-400°F (190-200°C) for a conventional oven, Gas Mark 5-6.

2 In a large bowl, sift together: flour, baking powder, salt, spice and sugar.

3 In another bowl, beat egg with a fork. Stir in chopped apple and milk, followed by oil/melted butter.

4 Pour all of wet mixture into dry. Stir just until combined, adding dried fruit/walnuts during the final strokes. This batter is thicker than most: apple releases juice as it cooks.

5 Spoon into tins. Sprinkle with topping. Bake about 20-25 minutes until tops are lightly browned and spring back when pressed gently. Cool for several minutes to make removal easier.

APRICOT ALMOND MUFFINS

Toasted almonds and apricots make a wonderful combination.

Makes 10-12 standard-size

9 oz (255 g) plain flour*
2¹/₂ teaspoons (12.5 ml) baking powder
¹/₄ teaspoon (1.2 ml) bicarbonate of soda
¹/₂ teaspoon (2.5 ml) salt
2 oz (60 g) toasted flaked almonds (instructions given below)
1 egg
4-5 oz (110-140 g) fine white granulated sugar or light
  brown soft sugar
1 teaspoon (5 ml) vanilla essence/flavouring
6 oz (170 g) ready-to-eat dried apricots, chopped
8-9 fl oz (240-260 ml) milk
3 fl oz (90 ml) vegetable oil or 3 oz (85 g) butter, melted

Method

1 Prepare muffin tins. Preheat oven to 375-400°F
   (190-200°C) for a conventional oven, Gas Mark 5-6.
2 To toast flaked almonds: spread on a baking sheet and bake
   for about 5 minutes until lightly browned.
3 In a large bowl, sift together: flour, baking powder,
   bicarbonate of soda and salt. Stir in toasted almonds.
4 In another bowl, beat egg with a fork. Stir in sugar, vanilla,
   chopped apricots, milk and oil/melted butter.
5 Pour all of wet mixture into dry. Stir just until combined and
   no dry flour is visible. Batter will be lumpy.
6 Fill muffin cups three-quarters full. Bake for 20-25 minutes,
   until tops are lightly browned and feel quite firm when
   pressed gently.

*With self-raising flour, reduce baking powder to 1 teaspoon (5 ml); do not
adjust bicarbonate of soda.*

BANANA MUFFINS

A perennial favourite that never fails to please!

Makes 11-12 standard-size

10 oz (280 g) plain flour*
1 teaspoon (5 ml) baking powder
1 teaspoon (5 ml) bicarbonate of soda
¹/₂ teaspoon (2.5 ml) salt
3 large well-ripened bananas (about 1 pound/450 g in total)
   will yield 8-10 fl oz/240-290 ml when peeled and mashed
4 oz (110 g) fine white granulated sugar
1 egg, beaten with a fork
2-3 fl oz (60-90 ml) milk or water
3 fl oz (90 ml) vegetable oil or 3 oz (85 g) butter, melted
2-3 oz (60-85 g) walnuts or plain chocolate chips (optional)

Method

1 Prepare muffin tins. Preheat oven to 375-400°F
   (190-200°C) for a conventional oven, Gas Mark 5-6.
2 In a large bowl, sift together: flour, baking powder,
   bicarbonate of soda and salt. (Add chocolate if using.)
3 In another bowl, mash bananas thoroughly with a potato
   masher. Stir in sugar, egg, milk/water and oil/butter.
   (Add oats and vanilla if using.)
4 Pour all of wet ingredients into dry. Stir just until batter is
   evenly mixed but still lumpy. No dry flour should be visible.
   (Add walnuts during the final strokes, if using.)
5 Spoon into tins. Bake for 20-25 minutes, until tops are
   lightly browned and spring back when pressed gently.

With self-raising flour, omit baking powder; do not alter bicarbonate of soda.

Note: Ripe bananas can be frozen in an air-tight container or freezer
bag. Simply thaw and peel when needed; though black and unappetizing,
they are perfect for baking!

Banana Oatmeal Muffins
Reduce flour to 8 oz (225 g). Add 2 oz (60 g) rolled oats to the
wet mixture. Add 1 teaspoon (5 ml) vanilla essence if desired.

BRAN MUFFINS

Cultured buttermilk is a low-fat product that gives a special flavour and tenderness in baking. These are full of fibre and a pleasure to eat! (If you need to use regular milk or water in place of buttermilk, see note below.)

Makes 11-12 standard-size

8 oz (225 g) plain flour
1 teaspoon (5 ml) bicarbonate of soda
$^1/_2$ teaspoon (2.5 ml) salt
1 egg
4-6 oz (110-170 g) soft brown sugar
1-2 Tablespoons (15-30 ml) black treacle or molasses or honey
2$^1/_2$ oz (75 g) natural wheat bran or 3$^1/_2$ oz (105 g) oat bran
8 fl oz (240 ml) cultured buttermilk
3 Tablespoons (45 ml) water
3 fl oz (90 ml) vegetable oil or 3 oz (85 g) butter, melted
3 oz (85 g) raisins, sultanas or chopped dates (optional)

Method

1 Prepare muffin tins. Preheat oven to 375-400°F (190-200°C) for a conventional oven, Gas Mark 5-6.
2 In a large bowl, sift together: flour, bicarbonate of soda and salt.
3 In a medium-sized bowl, beat egg with a fork. Stir in sugar, treacle/molasses/honey, bran, buttermilk, water and oil/butter.
4 Pour all of wet mixture into dry. Stir just until combined, adding dried fruit during the final strokes. Batter will be lumpy but no dry flour should be visible.
5 Spoon into tins. Bake 20-25 minutes, until tops spring back when pressed gently. Serve warm, with or without butter.

Note: When replacing buttermilk with either milk or water, omit bicarbonate of soda and use 3 teaspoons (15 ml) baking powder instead. You will probably not need the extra 3 Tablespoons of water.

Cheddar Bran Muffins
Add 2 oz (60 g) grated cheese to the dry ingredients.

BRAN CINNAMON MUFFINS

These are a real treat and a wonderful way to get bran into your family's diet! If you're in a hurry, the filling can simply be added to the batter instead of layering it.

Makes 10-11 standard-size

3 oz (85 g) bran cereal sticks
10 fl oz (290 ml) milk
7 oz (200 g) plain flour
3 teaspoons (15 ml) baking powder
$^1/_2$ teaspoon (2.5 ml) salt
1 egg, beaten with a fork
3 oz (85 g) light brown soft sugar
3 fl oz (90 ml) vegetable oil or 3 oz (85 g) butter, melted

Filling:
3 oz (85 g) light brown soft sugar
2 teaspoons (10 ml) ground cinnamon
3 oz (85 g) sultanas or raisins

Method

1 Prepare muffin tins. Preheat oven to 375-400°F (190-200°C) for a conventional oven, Gas Mark 5-6.
2 Stir together filling ingredients and set aside.
3 Combine bran cereal sticks and milk; set aside to soak for about 15 minutes. Meanwhile, in a large bowl, sift together: flour, baking powder and salt. Set aside.
4 Now to the bran mixture add beaten egg, sugar and oil/butter.
5 Pour all of wet mixture into dry. Stir just until evenly mixed but still lumpy.
6 Using about half the batter, spoon a small amount into each prepared cup. Cover with filling, and finish with remaining batter. Bake for 20-25 minutes, until tops spring back when pressed gently. For an extra treat, drizzle with maple syrup while hot.

BUTTERMILK MUFFINS

Although its name might suggest otherwise, cultured buttermilk is a low-fat product. These are delicious served warm with jam. For a fun alternative, try baking them with the jam already inside (as I did for the photo)!

Makes 10-11 standard-size

10 oz (280 g) plain flour*
1 teaspoon (5 ml) bicarbonate of soda
1/2 teaspoon (2.5 ml) salt
2-3 oz (60-85 g) fine white granulated sugar
1 egg
8 fl oz (240 ml) cultured buttermilk
2 fl oz (60 ml) water
3 fl oz (90 ml) vegetable oil or 3 oz (85 g) butter, melted

Method

1 Prepare muffin tins. Preheat oven to 375-400°F (190-200°C) for a conventional oven, Gas Mark 5-6.
2 In a large bowl, sift together: flour, bicarbonate of soda, salt and sugar.
3 In a separate bowl, beat egg with a fork. Stir in buttermilk and water, followed by oil/melted butter.
4 Pour all of wet ingredients into dry, and stir just until combined. Batter will be thick and lumpy, but no dry flour should be visible. Do not over-stir.
5 Spoon immediately into tins. (For a jam-filled centre, spoon half the batter into the tins, add a dollop of your favourite jam, and cover with remaining batter.) Bake for 20-25 minutes, until tops are lightly browned and spring back when pressed gently. Serve plain muffins warm with jam or butter.

This recipe is not suitable for self-raising flour.

BUTTERSCOTCH RAISIN MUFFINS

Full of flavour and crunch. A real treat! As with any muffin, adjust the sugar to suit your taste.

Makes 10-12 standard-size

9 oz (255 g) plain flour*
2 teaspoons (10 ml) baking powder
1/2 teaspoon (2.5 ml) bicarbonate of soda
1/2 teaspoon (2.5 ml) salt
1 egg
3-5 oz (85-140 g) soft brown or fine white granulated sugar
8 fl oz (240 ml) milk
2 teaspoons (10 ml) vanilla essence/flavouring
3 oz (85 g) butter, melted
4-5 oz (110-140 g) raisins or sultanas
2 oz (60 g) walnuts or pecans, chopped
Golden syrup, maple syrup or North American "corn syrup" for optional topping

Method

1 Prepare muffin tins. Preheat oven to 375-400°F (190-200°C) for a conventional oven, Gas Mark 5-6.
2 In a large bowl, sift together: flour, baking powder, bicarbonate of soda and salt.
3 In another bowl, beat egg with a fork. Add sugar, milk and vanilla, followed by melted butter.
4 Pour all of wet mixture into dry. Stir just until combined and no dry flour is visible. Add raisins and nuts during the final strokes.
5 Fill muffin cups three-quarters full. Bake for 20-25 minutes, until tops are lightly browned and feel quite firm. Spread a small spoonful of syrup over each muffin top: the syrup will soak into a hot muffin or make a shiny glaze on a cold muffin.

If using self-raising flour, omit baking powder; do not adjust bicarbonate of soda.

CARROT MUFFINS

So moist and delicious, and they don't taste at all like carrots!
These have much less sugar and oil than traditional carrot cake.
The icing is optional, of course.

Makes 10-12 standard-size

10 oz (280 g) plain flour*
1 teaspoon (5 ml) baking powder
1 teaspoon (5 ml) bicarbonate of soda
$^1/_2$ teaspoon (2.5 ml) salt
2 teaspoons (10 ml) ground cinnamon
1 egg
2-3 fl oz (60-90 ml) milk or water
2 Tablespoons (30 ml) honey
4-5 oz (110-140 g) fine white granulated sugar or light
   brown soft sugar
12 oz (340 g) carrot, finely grated (or chopped in a food
   processor)
1 teaspoon (5 ml) vanilla essence/flavouring
3 fl oz (90 ml) vegetable oil or 3 oz (85 g) butter, melted
2-3 oz (60-85 g) chopped walnuts or raisins (optional)

Icing (traditional with carrot cake):
2 oz (60 g) cream cheese, softened (at room temperature)
4 oz (110 g) icing sugar, sifted
$^1/_2$ teaspoon (2.5 ml) vanilla essence/flavouring

With self-raising flour, omit baking powder; do not adjust bicarbonate of soda.

Method

1 Prepare muffin tins. Preheat oven to 375-400°F
  (190-200°C) for a conventional oven, Gas Mark 5-6.
2 In a large bowl, sift together: flour, baking powder, bicarbonate
  of soda, salt and cinnamon. (Stir in bran, if using.)
3 In a separate bowl, beat egg with a fork. Add milk/water,
  honey, sugar, carrot and vanilla, followed by oil/melted
  butter. Stir well.
4 Pour all of liquid mixture into dry. Stir just until combined,
  adding walnuts/raisins during the final strokes. Do not
  over-stir.
5 Spoon into tins. Bake for 20-25 minutes, until tops spring
  back when pressed gently. Allow muffins to cool before
  icing. Stir icing ingredients together until blended.
  (Add $^1/_2$ teaspoon milk if needed.)

Carrot Bran Muffins
Decrease flour to 8 oz (225 g); add 1$^1/_4$ oz (40 g) wheat bran or
1$^3/_4$ oz (50 g) oat bran to the dry ingredients.

CHERRY WALNUT MUFFINS

An appealing mix of flavours and colours.

Makes 10-11 standard-size

9 oz (255 g) plain flour*
3 teaspoons (15 ml) baking powder
1/2 teaspoon (2.5 ml) salt
4 oz (110 g) fine white granulated sugar
1 egg
8-9 fl oz (240-260 ml) milk
4 oz (110 g) chopped glacé cherries
1/2 teaspoon (2.5 ml) almond essence/flavouring
3 fl oz (90 ml) vegetable oil or 3 oz (85 g) butter, melted
3 oz (85 g) chopped walnuts

Method

1 Prepare muffin tins. Preheat oven to 375-400°F (190-200°C) for a conventional oven, Gas Mark 5-6.
2 In a large bowl, sift together: flour, baking powder, salt and sugar.
3 In a separate bowl, beat egg with a fork. Stir in milk, followed by cherries, almond flavouring and oil/melted butter.
4 Pour all of liquid ingredients into dry mixture. Stir just until combined, adding walnuts during the final strokes. The batter will be lumpy, but no dry flour should be visible.
5 Fill muffin cups three-quarters full. Bake for 20-25 minutes until tops are lightly browned and spring back when pressed gently.

With self-raising flour, decrease baking powder to 1 teaspoon (5 ml).

CARROT PINEAPPLE MUFFINS

These are moist and scrumptious. Vary the flavour by including one or more of the optional additions.

Makes 11-12 standard-size

7 oz (200 g) carrot, finely grated (or chopped by food processor)
4 fl oz (120 ml) well-drained crushed pineapple (or 4 slices chopped)
9 oz (255 g) plain flour*
1 teaspoon (5 ml) baking powder
1 teaspoon (5 ml) bicarbonate of soda
1/2 teaspoon (2.5 ml) salt
2 teaspoons (10 ml) ground cinnamon
1 egg
4 oz (110 g) fine white granulated sugar or soft brown sugar
3-4 fl oz (90-120 ml) milk or water
3 fl oz (90 ml) vegetable oil or 3 oz (85 g) butter, melted

Optional Additions:
Walnuts, raisins, sultanas, desiccated coconut

Method

1 Prepare muffin tins. Preheat oven to 375-400°F (190-200°C) for a conventional oven, Gas Mark 5-6.
2 Prepare grated carrot and crushed pineapple. Set aside.
3 In a large bowl, sift together: flour, baking powder, bicarbonate of soda, salt and cinnamon.
4 In a medium-sized bowl, beat egg with a fork. Add sugar, milk/water, grated carrot, crushed pineapple and oil/butter.
5 Pour all of wet ingredients into dry. Stir just until combined, adding extra bits during the final strokes. Batter will be thick and lumpy.
6 Spoon into tins. Bake for 20-25 minutes, until tops feel quite firm. (Spread cooled muffins with cream cheese icing, page 22, if desired.)

With self-raising flour omit baking powder; do not omit bicarbonate of soda.

COLATE MUFFINS

Always a hit! These can be as sweet and chocolatey (or not!) as you like. Use butter for a richer flavour and oil for a lighter one. Enjoy the delicious variations as well . . .

Makes 10-11 standard-size

9 oz (255 g) plain flour*
2 teaspoons (10 ml) baking powder
1/2 teaspoon (2.5 ml) bicarbonate of soda
1/2 teaspoon (2.5 ml) salt
4-6 oz (110-170 g) fine white granulated sugar
3-5 Tablespoons (45-75 ml) unsweetened cocoa powder
1 egg
8-9 fl oz (240-260 ml) milk
1 teaspoon (5 ml) vanilla essence/flavouring
3 fl oz (90 ml) vegetable oil or 3 oz (85 g) butter, melted
Plain chocolate chips, coconut or chopped nuts for topping
    (optional)

Method

1 Prepare muffin tins. Preheat oven to 375-400°F (190-200°C) for a conventional oven, Gas Mark 5-6.

2 In a large bowl, sift together flour, baking powder, bicarbonate of soda, salt, sugar and cocoa powder.

3 In another bowl, beat egg with a fork. Stir in milk and vanilla, followed by oil/melted butter.

4 Pour all of wet mixture into dry. Stir just until combined and no dry flour is visible. Batter will be lumpy.

5 Fill muffin cups three-quarters full. Sprinkle tops with chocolate chips, coconut or nuts (or all three!). Bake for 20-25 minutes, until tops spring back when pressed gently.

With self-raising flour, omit baking powder; do not adjust bicarbonate of soda.

CHOCOLATE MUFFIN VARIATIONS

Chocolate Cheesecake Muffins
Stir together 4 oz (110 g) softened cream cheese and 3 Tablespoons (45 ml) caster (fine granulated) sugar; set aside. Prepare chocolate batter. Using about half the batter, spoon a small amount into each muffin cup. Drop about a teaspoon of cream cheese filling on top, and then finish with remaining chocolate batter. Bake as usual.

Chocolate Cherry Muffins
Add 3-4 oz (85-110 g) chopped glacé cherries or black cherries.

Chocolate Hazelnut Muffins
Add 2 oz (60 g) ground or chopped hazelnuts to the dry ingredients. Of course, any chopped nuts would go well with chocolate: pecans, walnuts, Brazil nuts, macadamia nuts, etc.

Chocolate Mocha Muffins
Prepare 8-9 fl oz (240-260 ml) strong black coffee. Cool completely and use in place of milk. For extra flavour, add a small amount of coffee flavouring.

Chocolate Orange Muffins
Add approximately 1 teaspoon (5 ml) finely grated orange rind to the wet ingredients.

Chocolate Muffins with a Quick Icing
Combine the following icing ingredients, stirring till smooth after each addition:
1 Tablespoon (15 ml) hot melted butter
1 Tablespoon (15 ml) unsweetened cocoa powder
1 1/2 Tablespoons (22 ml) boiling water
4 oz (110 g) icing sugar, sifted
1/2 teaspoon (2.5 ml) vanilla essence/flavouring
This icing thickens as it cools. Thin with a few drops of water if needed.

Double Chocolate Muffins
Add 3 oz (85 g) plain chocolate chips to the dry ingredients.

CINNAMON CRUNCH MUFFINS

Layering the batter with a mixture of cinnamon, nuts and sugar gives that extra-special look and taste. The amount of filling specified here will give a fine ribbon effect; this can be increased if desired.

Makes 11-12 standard-size

10 oz (280 g) plain flour*
2 teaspoons (10 ml) baking powder
1/2 teaspoon (2.5 ml) bicarbonate of soda
1/2 teaspoon (2.5 ml) salt
2 oz (60 g) fine white granulated sugar
1 egg
5 fl oz (150 ml) cultured sour cream
6 fl oz (180 ml) milk or water
2 fl oz (60 ml) vegetable oil
1 teaspoon (5 ml) vanilla essence/flavouring

For Filling and Topping:
3 oz (85 g) light brown soft sugar
3 oz (85 g) pecans or walnuts, chopped
2 teaspoons (10 ml) ground cinnamon

*With self-raising flour omit baking powder; do not omit bicarbonate of soda.

Method

1 Prepare muffin tins. Preheat oven to 375-400°F (190-200°C) for a conventional oven, Gas Mark 5-6.
2 Combine topping ingredients and set aside.
3 In a large bowl, sift together: flour, baking powder, bicarbonate of soda, salt and sugar.
4 In a separate bowl, beat egg with a fork. Stir in sour cream, milk/water, oil and vanilla.
5 Pour all of liquid mixture into dry. Stir just until combined and no dry flour is visible. Batter will be lumpy.
6 Using approximately half the batter, spoon a small amount into each cup. Sprinkle with half the cinnamon mixture. Spoon out remaining batter and finish with topping. Bake for 20-25 minutes, until tops spring back when pressed gently.

COCOA COURGETTE MUFFINS

Don't let the name put you off! As with carrot muffins, the courgette ("zucchini" in North America) simply adds moisture and vitamins. (These are really good. Honest!)

Makes 11-12 standard-size

10 oz (280 g) plain flour*
2 teaspoons (10 ml) baking powder
1/2 teaspoon (2.5 ml) bicarbonate of soda
1/2 teaspoon (2.5 ml) salt
2 teaspoons (10 ml) ground cinnamon
3 Tablespoons (45 ml) unsweetened cocoa powder
1 egg
4-5 oz (110-140 g) light brown soft sugar
2-3 fl oz (60-90 ml) milk or water
2 teaspoons (10 ml) vanilla essence/flavouring
12 oz (340 g) courgette, finely grated (or chopped in a food processor), which will yield about 16 fl oz (450 ml) when packed into a measuring jug – no need to peel the courgette, unless you want to avoid green flecks in the finished muffin
3 fl oz (90 ml) vegetable oil or 3 oz (85 g) butter, melted
3 oz (85 g) raisins or sultanas (optional)

Method

1 Prepare muffin tins. Preheat oven to 375-400°F (190-200°C) for a conventional oven, Gas Mark 5-6.
2 In a large bowl, sift together flour, baking powder, bicarbonate of soda, salt, cinnamon and cocoa powder.
3 In a medium-sized bowl, beat egg with a fork. Add sugar, milk/water, vanilla, courgette and oil/melted butter. Stir well.
4 Pour all of wet mixture into dry. Stir just until combined, adding dried fruit during the final strokes. Batter will be lumpy but no dry flour should be visible.
5 Spoon into tins. Bake for 20-25 minutes, until tops spring back when pressed gently.

If using self-raising flour, omit baking powder; do not adjust bicarbonate of soda.

CORNMEAL MUFFINS

So versatile, this muffin can work as a savoury or sweet: serve with or without butter to accompany a light meal such as soup, or serve with maple syrup to make a tasty dessert. Cornmeal is available in many delicatessens and speciality food shops.

Makes 10-11 standard-size

6 oz (170 g) plain flour*
3 teaspoons (15 ml) baking powder
1/2 teaspoon (2.5 ml) salt
2-3 oz (60-85 g) fine white granulated sugar
6 oz (170 g) yellow cornmeal
1 egg
8-10 fl oz (240-290 ml) milk
3 oz (85 g) butter, melted or 3 fl oz (90 ml) vegetable oil

Method

1 Prepare muffin tins. Preheat oven to 375-400°F (190-200°C) for a conventional oven, Gas Mark 5-6.
2 In a large bowl, sift together: flour, baking powder, salt and sugar. Stir in cornmeal.
3 In another bowl, beat egg with a fork. Add milk and melted butter/oil.
4 Pour all of wet ingredients into dry. Stir just until combined. Batter will be lumpy but no dry flour should be visible. Do not over-stir.
5 Spoon into tins. Bake for about 20 minutes, until edges appear golden brown and tops feel quite firm. Best served warm, with or without butter.

With self-raising flour, reduce baking powder to 2 teaspoons (10 ml).

Cornbread
Bake in a well-greased 8 or 9-inch (20-22.5cm) square cake tin for about 30-40 minutes, until lightly browned and firm to touch. Test for doneness by inserting a metal skewer or knife into the centre: it should come out clean.

Optional Savoury Additions:
Grated cheddar cheese, very finely chopped peppers or onion.

CRANBERRY MUFFINS

A tasty muffin, using ready-made sauce. To use fresh cranberries, see the variations given below and on page 44.

Makes 10-12 standard-size

10 oz (280 g) plain flour*
3 teaspoons (15 ml) baking powder
¹/₂ teaspoon (2.5 ml) salt
3-4 oz (85-110 g) fine white granulated sugar
1 egg
6 fl oz (180 ml) ready-made cranberry sauce (about 200 g), preferably with whole berries rather than smooth
¹/₂ teaspoon (2.5 ml) finely grated orange or lemon rind
5 fl oz (150 ml) milk
3 fl oz (90 ml) vegetable oil or 3 oz (85 g) butter, melted
2 oz (60 g) pecans or walnuts, chopped (optional)

Method

1 Prepare muffin tins. Preheat oven to 375-400°F (190-200°C) for a conventional oven, Gas Mark 5-6.
2 In a large bowl, sift together: flour, baking powder, salt and sugar.
3 In a separate bowl, beat egg with a fork. Stir in cranberry sauce, grated orange or lemon rind, milk and oil/melted butter.
4 Pour all of liquid ingredients into dry. Stir just until combined, adding nuts during the final strokes. Batter will be lumpy but no dry flour should be visible.
5 Spoon into tins. Bake for 20-25 minutes, until tops are lightly browned and spring back when pressed gently.

With self-raising flour, decrease baking powder to 1 teaspoon (5 ml).

Fresh Cranberry Muffins
Use 4 oz (110 g) coarsely chopped fresh cranberries instead of cranberry sauce. Increase milk to 8 fl oz (240 ml).

DATE WALNUT MUFFINS

A classic combination and an excellent muffin.

Makes 10-12 standard-size

10 fl oz (290 ml) boiling water
6 oz (170 g) dried stoned dates, chopped
10 oz (280 g) plain flour*
2 teaspoons (10 ml) baking powder
¹/₂ teaspoon (2.5 ml) bicarbonate of soda
¹/₂ teaspoon (2.5 ml) salt
1 egg
4 oz (110 g) light brown soft sugar
1 teaspoon (5 ml) vanilla essence/flavouring
3 fl oz (90 ml) vegetable oil or 3 oz (85 g) butter, melted
3 oz (85 g) walnuts, chopped

Method

1 Prepare boiling water and pour over chopped dates. Set aside to soak and cool for approximately 30 minutes. Do not discard water.
2 Prepare muffin tins. Preheat oven to 375-400°F (190-200°C) for a conventional oven, Gas Mark 5-6.
3 In a large bowl, sift together: flour, baking powder, bicarbonate of soda and salt.
4 In a separate bowl, beat egg with a fork. Stir in sugar, vanilla, cooled water and date mixture, and oil/melted butter.
5 Pour all of liquid ingredients into dry mixture. Stir just until combined, adding walnuts during the final strokes.
6 Spoon into tins. Bake for 20-25 minutes, until tops spring back when pressed gently.

With self-raising flour, omit baking powder; do not adjust bicarbonate of soda.

Coffee Date-Walnut Muffins
Soak dates in 10 fl oz strong hot coffee instead of water. Cool and combine as usual. For an optional topping, sprinkle with a mixture of 2 oz (60 g) brown sugar and ¹/₂ teaspoon (2.5 ml) cinnamon before baking.

GINGERBREAD MUFFINS

We especially enjoy these served warm with fresh applesauce, with or without a drizzle of cream!

Makes 10-11 standard-size

9 oz (255 g) plain flour
1½ teaspoons (7.5 ml) baking powder
½ teaspoon (2.5 ml) bicarbonate of soda
½ teaspoon (2.5 ml) salt
1½ teaspoons (7.5 ml) ground ginger
1 teaspoon (5 ml) ground cinnamon
¼ teaspoon (1.2 ml) ground nutmeg
1 egg
4-6 oz (110-170 g) soft brown sugar
2-3 Tablespoons (30-45 ml) black treacle or light molasses (apply some vegetable oil to your spoon first to make this easier)
6 fl oz (180 ml) milk
3 fl oz (90 ml) vegetable oil or 3 oz (85 g) butter, melted

Optional Additions:
Raisins, chopped crystallized ginger

*With self-raising flour, omit baking powder; do not adjust bicarbonate of soda.

Method

1 Prepare muffin tins. Preheat oven to 375-400°F (190-200°C) for a conventional oven, Gas Mark 5-6.
2 In a large bowl, sift together flour, baking powder, bicarbonate of soda, salt, ginger, cinnamon and nutmeg.
3 In a separate bowl, beat egg with a fork and stir in brown sugar. Warm treacle/molasses slightly before adding; stir in with a fork until blended. Add milk and oil/melted butter and continue to stir briskly until well mixed.
4 Pour all of wet mixture into dry and stir to combine. This requires slightly more stirring than other muffin batters due to the sticky nature of treacle. The batter will also appear thinner and smoother.
5 Spoon into tins. Bake for 20-25 minutes, until tops feel quite firm. Best served warm.

For fresh applesauce: peel and slice two large cooking apples into a saucepan with a small amount of water and simmer for 10-15 minutes until soft. Mash apples and water together, adding extra water if needed. Add caster sugar to taste.

MUFFINS

So simple, so good! If you prefer to omit the glaze, you might like to add lemon flavouring to the batter for extra flavour.

Makes 9-11 standard-size

9 oz (255 g) plain flour*
3 teaspoons (15 ml) baking powder
1/2 teaspoon (2.5 ml) salt
3-4 oz (85-110 g) fine white granulated sugar
1 egg
8 fl oz (240 ml) milk
1 teaspoon (5 ml) finely grated lemon rind
3 fl oz (90 ml) vegetable oil or 3 oz (85 g) butter, melted
1/2 teaspoon (2.5 ml) lemon flavouring (optional)

Optional Glaze:
3 oz (85 g) icing sugar, sifted
3-4 teaspoons (15-20 ml) fresh lemon juice
1/4 teaspoon (1.2 ml) grated lemon rind

With self-raising flour, reduce baking powder to 1 teaspoon (5 ml).

Method

1 Prepare muffin tins. Preheat oven to 375-400°F (190-200°C) for a conventional oven, Gas Mark 5-6.
2 In a large bowl, sift together: flour, baking powder, salt and sugar. (Add poppy seeds if using.)
3 In a separate bowl, beat egg with a fork. Stir in milk, followed by grated lemon rind and oil/butter. (Add lemon flavouring if using.)
4 Pour all of liquid ingredients into dry mixture. Stir just until combined. (Add raisins/sultanas if using.) Batter will be lumpy but no dry flour should be visible.
5 Spoon into tins. Bake for 20-25 minutes, until tops are lightly browned and spring back when pressed gently. Spread immediately with glaze so that it melts over the hot muffins.

Lemon Poppy Seed Muffins
Add 1-2 Tablespoons (15-30 ml) poppy seeds to the dry ingredients.

Lemon Raisin Muffins
Add 3 oz (85 g) raisins or sultanas. Increase liquid by 1-2 Tablespoons (15-30 ml).

MAPLE PECAN MUFFINS

A Canadian classic . . . and with the goodness of oats!

Makes 10-11 standard-size

1 egg
8 fl oz (240 ml) milk
3 fl oz (90 ml) pure maple syrup
2 oz (60 g) rolled oats
3 oz (85 g) butter or suitable margarine, softened (not melted)
3 oz (85 g) fine white granulated sugar
8 oz (225 g) plain flour*
3 teaspoons (15 ml) baking powder
$^1/_2$ teaspoon (2.5 ml) salt
2-3 oz (60-85 g) pecans or walnuts, chopped

Optional Glaze:
1 rounded Tablespoon butter, softened (not melted)
2 oz (60 g) icing sugar, sifted
1 Tablespoon (15 ml) maple syrup (plus $^1/_2$ teaspoon milk
  if needed)

With self-raising flour, reduce baking powder to 1 teaspoon (5 ml).

Method

1 Prepare muffin tins. Preheat oven to 375-400°F (190-200°C) for a conventional oven, Gas Mark 5-6.
2 In a medium-sized bowl, beat egg with a fork. Add milk, maple syrup and rolled oats. Set aside to soak while you prepare the rest of the ingredients.
3 In a large bowl, blend together soft butter and sugar with a spoon.
4 Sift together: flour, baking powder and salt. Add to the butter mixture and cut in with a pastry blender (or rub lightly with fingers) until it resembles fine crumbs.
5 Pour all of wet mixture into dry. Stir just until combined, adding nuts during the final strokes. Do not over-stir.
6 Spoon into tins. Bake for 20-25 minutes, until tops are lightly browned and feel quite firm. Stir glaze ingredients together until smooth. Spread thinly on hot muffin tops immediately after baking.

MINCEMEAT SULTANA MUFFINS

Loaded with plump juicy sultanas, these are a treat at any time of year!

Makes 11-12 standard-size

10 oz (280 g) plain flour*
2 teaspoons (10 ml) baking powder
1/2 teaspoon (2.5 ml) bicarbonate of soda
1/2 teaspoon (2.5 ml) salt
3 oz (85 g) fine white granulated sugar
1 egg
8 fl oz (240 ml) milk
8 fl oz (240 ml) ready-made mincemeat (about 12 oz/350 g)
3 fl oz (90 ml) vegetable oil or 3 oz (85 g) butter, melted
3 oz (85 g) sultanas
Icing sugar for dusting the tops (optional)

Method

1 Prepare muffin tins. Preheat oven to 375-400°F (190-200°C) for a conventional oven, Gas Mark 5-6.
2 In a large bowl, sift together: flour, baking powder, bicarbonate of soda, salt and sugar.
3 In a separate bowl, beat egg with a fork. Stir in milk, mincemeat and oil/melted butter.
4 Pour all of liquid ingredients into dry mixture. Stir just until combined, adding the sultanas during the final strokes. The batter will be lumpy, but no dry flour should be visible. Do not over-stir.
5 Fill muffin cups three-quarters full. Bake for 20-25 minutes until tops are lightly browned and spring back when pressed gently. Allow muffins to cool for several minutes to make removal easier. Sieve icing sugar over tops.

With self-raising flour, omit baking powder; do not adjust bicarbonate of soda.

MARMALADE APRICOT MUFFINS

A warm blend of flavours, this makes an excellent morning muffin. If using a whole orange rather than ready-made juice, the zest can be added for extra flavour.

Makes 11-12 standard-size

10 oz (280 g) plain flour*
1 1/2 teaspoons (7.5 ml) baking powder
1/2 teaspoon (2.5 ml) bicarbonate of soda
1/2 teaspoon (2.5 ml) salt
3-4 oz (85-110 g) fine white granulated sugar
1 egg
1/2 teaspoon (2.5 ml) finely grated orange rind (optional)
3 fl oz (90 ml) pure orange juice
3-4 fl oz (90-120 ml) milk or water
4 fl oz (120 ml) orange marmalade, warmed slightly to improve distribution in the batter
4 oz (110 g) ready-to-eat dried apricots, chopped
3 fl oz (90 ml) vegetable oil or 3 oz (85 g) butter, melted

Method

1 Prepare muffin tins. Preheat oven to 375-400°F (190-200°C) for a conventional oven, Gas Mark 5-6.
2 In a large bowl, sift together: flour, baking powder, bicarbonate of soda, salt and sugar.
3 In a separate bowl, beat egg with a fork. Add orange juice (and rind if using), milk/water, marmalade, apricots and oil/melted butter. Stir well.
4 Pour all of liquid ingredients into dry mixture. Stir just until combined. The batter will be lumpy but no dry flour should be visible.
5 Spoon immediately into tins. Bake for 20-25 minutes until tops are lightly browned and spring back when pressed gently.

With self-raising flour, omit baking powder; do not adjust bicarbonate of soda.

OATMEAL CHOCOLATE-CHIP MUFFINS

A popular flavour with a healthy twist. A great way to get oats into your family's diet! Berries or dried fruit can be substituted for the chocolate chips if you prefer.

Makes 10-11 standard-size

2 oz (60 g) rolled oats
9 fl oz (260 ml) milk
8 oz (225 g) plain flour*
3 teaspoons (15 ml) baking powder
1/2 teaspoon (2.5 ml) salt
3 oz (85 g) plain chocolate chips, either chopped or left whole
1 egg, beaten with a fork
3-4 oz (85-110 g) light brown soft sugar
1 teaspoon (5 ml) vanilla essence/flavouring
3 fl oz (90 ml) vegetable oil or 3 oz (85 g) butter, melted

With self-raising flour, reduce baking powder to 1 teaspoon (5 ml).

Method

1 Prepare muffin tins. Preheat oven to 375-400°F (190-200°C) for a conventional oven, Gas Mark 5-6.
2 In a medium-sized bowl, combine oats and milk. Set aside to soak while you prepare the dry ingredients.
3 In a large bowl, sift together: flour, baking powder and salt. Stir in chocolate chips.
4 Now to the milk and oat mixture, add beaten egg, sugar, vanilla and oil/melted butter. Stir well.
5 Pour all of wet mixture into the dry. Stir just until combined and no dry flour is visible. Batter will be lumpy; do not over-stir.
6 Fill muffin cups three-quarters full. Bake for 20-25 minutes, until tops are lightly browned and feel quite firm to touch.

OATMEAL YOGURT MUFFINS

Just as delicious as they are healthy. Try fresh berries such as cranberries or blueberries for a seasonal touch.

Makes 10-12 standard-size

7 oz (200 g) plain flour*
1¹/₂ teaspoons (7.5 ml) baking powder
¹/₂ teaspoon (2.5 ml) salt
3 oz (85 g) rolled oats
8 fl oz (240 ml) plain yogurt
1 teaspoon (5 ml) bicarbonate of soda
1 egg, beaten with a fork
4-5 oz (110-140 g) light brown soft sugar
3-4 fl oz (90-120 ml) milk
3 fl oz (90 ml) vegetable oil or 3 oz (85 g) butter, melted
3 oz (85 g) raisins or 5 oz (140 g) berries (Cranberries should be coarsely chopped. If using frozen berries, do not thaw; instead, bake the muffins for an extra few minutes.)

With self-raising flour, omit baking powder; do not adjust bicarbonate of soda.

Method

1 Prepare muffin tins. Preheat oven to 375-400°F (190-200°C) for a conventional oven, Gas Mark 5-6.
2 In a large bowl, sift together: flour, baking powder and salt. Set aside.
3 Do the following step just before baking: in a separate bowl, stir together oats, yogurt and bicarbonate of soda. Let this stand for a minute, then add beaten egg, sugar, milk and oil/butter. Stir well.
4 Pour all of wet mixture into the dry. Stir just until combined, adding fruit during the final strokes. Batter will be lumpy but no dry flour should be visible. Do not over-stir.
5 Spoon immediately into tins. Bake for 20-25 minutes, until tops are lightly browned and spring back when pressed gently.

ORANGE-CARROT SPICE MUFFINS

The orange-spice combination gives a delicious flavour while the carrot contributes moisture and vitamins. If you prefer to omit the sweet topping, the nuts can be added to the batter instead.

Makes 11-12 standard-size

10 oz (280 g) plain flour*
2 teaspoons (10 ml) baking powder
$^1/_2$ teaspoon (2.5 ml) bicarbonate of soda
$^1/_2$ teaspoon (2.5 ml) salt
$^1/_2$ teaspoon (2.5 ml) ground cinnamon
$^1/_4$ teaspoon (1.2 ml) each ground cloves and nutmeg
1 egg
3-4 oz (85-110 g) fine white granulated sugar
Finely grated rind of 1 large orange (1-2 teaspoons/5-10 ml)
   – avoid grating into the white pith which is bitter
Juice of the orange plus water to make a total of 6 fl oz
   (180 ml)
4 oz (110 g) carrot, finely grated (or chopped by food-
   processor)
3 fl oz (90 ml) vegetable oil or 3 oz (85 g) butter, melted
2-3 oz (60-85 g) raisins, sultanas or currants (optional)

Optional Topping:
3 Tablespoons (45 ml) light brown soft sugar
1 Tablespoon (15 ml) melted butter
2 oz (60 g) pecans or walnuts, chopped

With self-raising flour, omit baking powder; do not omit bicarbonate of soda.

Method

1 Prepare muffin tins. Preheat oven to 375-400°F (190-200°C) for a conventional oven, Gas Mark 5-6.
2 In a large bowl, sift together: flour, baking powder, bicarbonate of soda, salt and spices.
3 In a separate bowl, beat egg with a fork. Stir in sugar, grated orange rind, juice plus water, carrot and oil/melted butter.
4 Pour all of liquid ingredients into the dry mixture. Stir just until evenly mixed, adding dried fruit during the final strokes. Batter will be thick and lumpy.
5 Spoon into tins. Combine topping, and spoon over tops. Bake for 20-25 minutes, until tops spring back when pressed gently.

ORANGE MUFFINS

Delicious fresh orange flavour; use firm juicy oranges, not the tangerine type.

Makes 10-12 standard-size

10 oz (280 g) plain flour*
1¹/₂ teaspoons (7.5 ml) baking powder
¹/₂ teaspoon (2.5 ml) bicarbonate of soda
¹/₂ teaspoon (2.5 ml) salt
3-4 oz (85-110 g) fine white granulated sugar
1 egg
2-3 teaspoons (10-15 ml) finely grated orange rind
   (of 2 large oranges); avoid grating into the white pith
   which is bitter
Juice of both oranges (about 6 fl oz/180 ml) – first set aside
   enough for glaze; add water to remainder to make a total
   of 8 fl oz (240 ml)
3 fl oz (90 ml) vegetable oil or 3 oz (85 g) butter, melted

Optional Glaze:
3 oz (85 g) icing sugar, sifted
3-4 teaspoons (15-20 ml) orange juice
¹/₂ teaspoon (2.5 ml) finely grated orange rind

With self-raising flour, omit baking powder; do not omit bicarbonate of soda.

Method

1 Prepare muffin tins. Preheat oven to 375-400°F
   (190-200°C) for a conventional oven, Gas Mark 5-6.
2 In a large bowl, sift together: flour, baking powder,
   bicarbonate of soda, salt and sugar. (Add poppy seeds if
   using.)
3 In a separate bowl, beat egg with a fork. Add grated rind,
   juice (plus water) and oil/butter.
4 Pour all of wet mixture into dry. Stir just until combined.
   (Add dried fruit during the final strokes if using). Batter will
   be lumpy.
5 Spoon immediately into tins. Bake for 20-25 minutes, until
   tops are lightly browned and spring back when pressed
   gently. Combine glaze ingredients: as you stir, use the back
   of the spoon to press the flavourful oils from the grated rind.
   Spread glaze thinly over hot muffin tops.

Orange Poppy Seed Muffins
Add 1-2 Tablespoons (15-30 ml) poppy seeds to the dry
ingredients.

Orange Muffins with Dried Fruit
Add 3 oz (85 g) raisins, sultanas, chopped dates or prunes.
Increase liquid by 1-2 Tablespoons (15-30 ml).

PEACH OR RHUBARB MUFFINS

Fresh fruit is ideal for this recipe, but tinned or frozen fruit makes it possible to enjoy these out of season too. Summer berries also work well here. Likewise, peaches or rhubarb can be used in the Summer Fruit recipe on page 58.

Makes 10-12 standard-size

10 oz (280 g) plain flour*
2 teaspoons (10 ml) baking powder
¹/₂ teaspoon (2.5 ml) bicarbonate of soda
¹/₂ teaspoon (2.5 ml) salt
3-5 oz (85-140 g) fine white granulated sugar
1-2 oz (30-60 g) flaked almonds (optional)
1 egg
5 fl oz (150 ml) milk
5 fl oz (150 ml) cultured sour cream
¹/₂ teaspoon (2.5 ml) almond essence/flavouring
2 fl oz (60 ml) vegetable oil
5-6 oz (140-170 g) peaches or rhubarb, chopped (drain well if using tinned fruit; do not thaw frozen fruit)

Method

1 Prepare muffin tins. Preheat oven to 375-400°F (190-200°C) for a conventional oven, Gas Mark 5-6.
2 In a large bowl, sift together: flour, baking powder, bicarbonate of soda, salt and sugar. (Add almonds if using.)
3 In a separate bowl, beat egg with a fork. Stir in milk, sour cream, almond essence and oil.
4 Pour all of wet ingredients into dry. Stir just to combine, folding in fruit with the final strokes. Batter will be lumpy but no dry flour should be visible.
5 Spoon into muffin cups. Bake for 20-25 minutes. Frozen fruit will require a few extra minutes. Tops should be lightly browned and spring back when pressed gently.

With self-raising flour, omit baking powder; do not omit bicarbonate of soda.

ORANGE-DATE BRAN MUFFINS

This recipe is based on one developed many years ago by my English great-aunt living in Canada. These muffins, packed with nutrition, were a favourite snack food during my childhood. (Wheat germ is extremely nutritious; try adding a spoonful to all your baking!)

Makes 10-11 standard-size

7 oz (200 g) plain flour
1 teaspoon (5 ml) baking powder
1 teaspoon (5 ml) bicarbonate of soda
¹/₂ teaspoon (2.5 ml) salt
2¹/₂ oz (75 g) wheat bran or 3¹/₂ oz (105 g) oat bran
1¹/₂ oz (45 g) wheat germ
1 egg
Finely grated rind of 1 large orange (1-2 teaspoons/5-10 ml)
    – be careful not to grate into the white pith which is bitter
4-6 oz (110-170 g) light brown soft sugar
8-9 fl oz (240-260 ml) milk
3 fl oz (90 ml) vegetable oil or 3 oz (85 g) butter, melted
5 oz (140 g) dried dates, chopped

Method

1 Prepare muffin tins. Preheat oven to 375-400°F (190-200°C) for a conventional oven, Gas Mark 5-6.
2 Sift together flour, baking powder, bicarbonate of soda and salt. Add bran and wheat germ and mix with a fork.
3 In a separate bowl, beat egg with a fork. Add orange rind, sugar, milk and oil/melted butter.
4 Pour all of wet mixture into the dry. Stir just until combined, adding chopped dates during the final strokes.
5 Spoon into tins. Bake for 20-25 minutes. Tops should feel quite firm when touched. Cool for a few minutes to make removal easier. Serve warm, with or without butter.

With self-raising flour, omit baking powder; do not alter bicarbonate of soda.

PINEAPPLE MUFFINS

Moist and mild. Coconut makes an attractive tasty topping, and can also be added to the batter.

Makes 10-12 standard-size

10 oz (280 g) plain flour*
2¹/₂ teaspoons (12.5 ml) baking powder
¹/₄ teaspoon (1.2 ml) bicarbonate of soda
¹/₂ teaspoon (2.5 ml) salt
4 oz (110 g) fine white granulated sugar
1 egg
6-8 fl oz (180-240 ml) crushed pineapple – drain well
   before packing into a measuring jug (see note below)
7-8 fl oz (210-240 ml) milk
3 fl oz (90 ml) vegetable oil or 3 oz (85 g) butter, melted
Desiccated coconut for topping and batter, if desired

Method

1 Prepare muffin tins. Preheat oven to 375-400°F
   (190-200°C) for a conventional oven, Gas Mark 5-6.
2 In a large bowl, sift together: flour, baking powder,
   bicarbonate of soda, salt and sugar.
3 In a separate bowl, beat egg with a fork. Stir in well-drained
   pineapple, milk and oil/melted butter.
4 Pour all of wet ingredients into dry. Stir just to combine.
   Batter will be thick and lumpy but no dry flour should be
   visible.
5 Spoon into tins. Sprinkle with coconut. Bake for 20-25
   minutes, until tops are lightly browned and spring back
   when pressed gently.

Note: A 350-400 g tin of pineapple is sufficient. Use either ready-crushed pineapple or 6-8 slices (or the equivalent amount of chunks) well-chopped. Press out most of the juice and pack only the fruit into a measuring jug: this should yield 6-8 fl oz (180-240 ml) pineapple. Either discard the juice or use part milk and part juice in the liquid ingredients.

With self-raising flour, use 1 teaspoon (5 ml) baking powder; do not omit bicarbonate of soda.

PEAR GINGER MUFFINS

Delicious for snacks – or try them with ice cream or hot custard for a mouth-watering dessert! I like to use tinned pears in unsweetened pear juice for convenience and extra pear flavour.

Makes 11-12 standard-size

10 oz (280 g) plain flour*
2 teaspoons (10 ml) baking powder
¹/₂ teaspoon (2.5 ml) bicarbonate of soda
¹/₂ teaspoon (2.5 ml) salt
1¹/₂ teaspoons (7.5 ml) ground ginger
3-4 oz (85-110 g) fine white granulated sugar
1 egg
6 fl oz (180 ml) milk or unsweetened pear juice
6 oz (170 g) pear, well-chopped (either tinned or fresh
   ripe pear)
3 Tablespoons (45 ml) honey
3 fl oz (90 ml) vegetable oil or 3 oz (85 g) butter, melted
2 oz (60 g) hazelnuts or walnuts, chopped (optional)

Method

1 Prepare muffin tins. Preheat oven to 375-400°F
   (190-200°C) for a conventional oven, Gas Mark 5-6.
2 In a large bowl, sift together: flour, baking powder,
   bicarbonate of soda, salt, ginger and sugar.
3 In a separate bowl, beat egg with a fork. Add milk/juice,
   chopped pear, honey and oil/melted butter. Stir well.
4 Pour all of liquid ingredients into dry mixture. Stir just until
   combined, adding nuts during the final strokes if using.
   Batter will be lumpy but no dry flour should be visible.
5 Fill muffin cups three-quarters full. Bake for 20-25 minutes.
   Muffins are done when tops are lightly browned and spring
   back when pressed gently.

With self-raising flour, omit baking powder; do not adjust bicarbonate of soda.

PUMPKIN MUFFINS

These are always a hit! Pumpkin, a member of the squash family, is rich in Vitamin A and gives a wonderfully moist texture. If tinned pumpkin is unavailable, try using butternut squash instead. I guarantee you won't be able to tell the difference! (See note below.)

Makes 10-12 standard-size

9 oz (255 g) plain flour*
1 teaspoon (5 ml) baking powder
1 teaspoon (5 ml) bicarbonate of soda
1/2 teaspoon (2.5 ml) salt
1 teaspoon (5 ml) ground cinnamon
1/2 teaspoon (2.5 ml) each of ground ginger, nutmeg and cloves
4-6 oz (110-170 g) fine white granulated sugar
1 egg
3-4 fl oz (90-120 ml) milk or water
3 Tablespoons (45 ml) honey
Half of a 425 g tin of pumpkin – that is, 7 fl oz (200 ml) – the remainder can be frozen in an airtight container
3 fl oz (90 ml) vegetable oil or 3 oz (85 g) butter, melted
2-3 oz (60-85 g) chopped walnuts or raisins

Method

1 Prepare muffin tins. Preheat oven to 375-400°F (190-200°C) for a conventional oven, Gas Mark 5-6.
2 In a large bowl, sift together: flour, baking powder, bicarbonate of soda, salt, spices and sugar.
3 In a separate bowl, beat egg with a fork. Add milk/water, honey, pumpkin and oil/melted butter. Stir well.
4 Pour all of liquid mixture into dry. Stir just until combined and no dry flour is visible. Add walnuts/raisins during the final strokes.
5 Spoon batter into tins. Bake for 20-25 minutes, until tops spring back when pressed gently.

Note: Cut and peel squash, removing pulp and seeds. Cook chunks in simmering water for 15-20 minutes until soft. Drain and discard liquid; purée squash in a food processor. An 800 g squash will yield about 16 fl oz (500 ml) purée, enough for two batches.

With self-raising flour, omit baking powder; do not adjust bicarbonate of soda.

POPPY SEED MUFFINS

More than just "decoration", in this muffin poppy seeds give a unique taste, appearance, and texture.

Makes 10-11 standard-size

10 oz (280 g) plain flour*
2 teaspoons (10 ml) baking powder
1/2 teaspoon (2.5 ml) bicarbonate of soda
1/2 teaspoon (2.5 ml) salt
3-4 oz (85-110 g) fine white granulated sugar
4 Tablespoons (60 ml) poppy seeds
1 egg
5 fl oz (150 ml) cultured sour cream
6 fl oz (180 ml) milk or water
1 teaspoon (5 ml) almond essence/flavouring
2 fl oz (60 ml) vegetable oil or 2 oz (60 g) butter, melted

Method

1 Prepare muffin tins. Preheat oven to 375-400°F (190-200°C) for a conventional oven, Gas Mark 5-6.
2 In a large bowl, sift together: flour, baking powder, bicarbonate of soda, salt and sugar. Stir in poppy seeds.
3 In a separate bowl, beat egg with a fork. Stir in sour cream, milk/water, almond essence and oil/melted butter.
4 Pour all of liquid mixture into dry. Stir just until combined and no dry flour is visible. Do not over-stir.
5 Fill muffin cups three-quarters full. Bake for 20-25 minutes, until tops are lightly browned and spring back when pressed gently.

With self-raising flour, omit baking powder; do not adjust bicarbonate of soda.

SAVOURY CHEESE MUFFINS

A deliciously simple savoury muffin which can be adapted to suit any tastes! As the flavour possibilities are endless and taste is an individual thing, I felt it would be more useful to give a basic savoury recipe with guidelines for varying it. Two suggestions are given below, but you can also try experimenting with different kinds and combinations of cheese, herbs, and other savoury additions such as chopped peppers, olives, pickles, etc. A small amount of sugar is included to improve the texture of the muffin. These are best served fresh and warm.

Makes 9-10 standard-size

9 oz (255 g) plain flour*
3 teaspoons (15 ml) baking powder
$^1/_2$ teaspoon (2.5 ml) salt
2-3 Tablespoons (30-45 ml) fine white granulated sugar
3 oz (85 g) cheddar cheese (or other), grated
1 egg
8 fl oz (240 ml) milk
3 fl oz (90 ml) vegetable oil or 3 oz (85 g) butter, melted
Grated cheese or sesame seeds for optional topping

With self-raising flour, reduce baking powder to 1 teaspoon (5 ml).

Method

1 Prepare muffin tins. These tend to stick to the paper liners more than sweet muffins, so greasing might be preferable. Preheat oven to 375-400°F (190-200°C) for a conventional oven, Gas Mark 5-6.

2 In a large bowl, sift together: flour, baking powder, salt and sugar. Stir in grated cheese.

3 In another bowl, beat egg with a fork. Stir in milk, followed by oil/melted butter. (Add any additional bits if using.)

4 Pour all of wet ingredients into dry. Stir just until combined. Batter will be lumpy but no dry flour should be visible. Do not over-stir.

5 Spoon into tins. Sprinkle tops with extra cheese or sesame seeds if desired. Bake for 20-25 minutes, until tops are lightly browned and spring back when pressed gently. Cool for several minutes to make removal easier.

Cheese and Onion Muffins
Finely chop one small onion. Sauté in a small amount of oil until softened, and add to the wet ingredients.

Cheese and Herb Muffins
Add 2-3 Tablespoons (30-45 ml) chopped fresh basil, chives or other herbs, or about 1 teaspoon (5 ml) dried herbs.

SUMMER FRUIT MUFFINS

Enjoy these muffins year-round using fresh or frozen berries. Butter will give a richer flavour and oil a lighter one, or you might like to try a combination of the two for a compromise. Serve plain for a delicious snack or with cream for a mouth-watering dessert!

Makes 10-12 standard-size

10 oz (280 g) plain flour*
3 teaspoons (15 ml) baking powder
$^1/_2$ teaspoon (2.5 ml) salt
4-5 oz (110-140 g) fine white granulated sugar
1 egg
8 fl oz (240 ml) milk
3 fl oz (90 ml) vegetable oil or 3 oz (85 g) butter, melted
5-6 oz (140-170 g) summer fruit (any "berries", either alone or in combination: blueberries, raspberries, blackberries, strawberries, redcurrants, cherries, etc.), fresh or frozen – do not thaw frozen berries; larger-sized berries should be coarsely chopped

Method

1 Prepare muffin tins. Preheat oven to 375-400°F (190-200°C) for a conventional oven, Gas Mark 5-6.
2 In a large bowl, sift together: flour, baking powder, salt and sugar.
3 In another bowl, beat egg with a fork. Stir in milk, followed by oil/melted butter.
4 Pour all of wet ingredients into dry. Stir just to combine. Batter will be lumpy but no dry flour should be visible. Gently fold in berries at the end, using only a couple of strokes to avoid crushing the fruit.
5 Spoon into muffin cups. Bake for 20-25 minutes. Frozen fruit will require an extra 4-5 minutes. Muffins are done when tops are lightly browned and spring back when pressed gently.

With self-raising flour, reduce baking powder to 1 teaspoon (5 ml).

TROPICAL FRUIT MUFFINS

Moist and fruity, with a deliciously subtle blend of tropical flavours. For a non-dairy alternative, you could use either tinned coconut milk or pineapple juice.

Makes 12 standard-size

10 oz (280 g) plain flour*
2 teaspoons (10 ml) baking powder
$^1/_2$ teaspoon (2.5 ml) bicarbonate of soda
$^1/_2$ teaspoon (2.5 ml) salt
4 oz (110 g) fine white granulated sugar
2 oz (60 g) desiccated coconut
1 egg
5-6 fl oz (150-180 ml) milk
4 oz (110 g) pineapple (about 3 slices), chopped
1 large ripe banana, mashed
$^1/_4$ teaspoon (1.2 ml) finely grated lime rind (optional)
4 oz (110 g) fresh or dried mango, chopped (optional)
3 fl oz (90 ml) vegetable oil or 3 oz (85 g) butter, melted
Extra coconut for topping (optional)

Method

1 Prepare muffin tins. Preheat oven to 375-400°F (190-200°C) for a conventional oven, Gas Mark 5-6.
2 In a large bowl, sift together: flour, baking powder, bicarbonate of soda, salt and sugar. Stir in coconut.
3 In a separate bowl, beat egg with a fork. Stir in milk, pineapple, banana, grated lime rind, mango and oil/melted butter.
4 Pour all of wet ingredients into dry. Stir just to combine. Batter will be thick and lumpy but no dry flour should be visible.
5 Spoon into tins. Sprinkle with extra coconut if desired. Bake for 20-25 minutes, until tops are lightly browned and spring back when pressed gently.

With self-raising flour, omit baking powder; do not alter bicarbonate of soda.

APPENDIX 1

GLUTEN-FREE AND WHEAT-FREE MUFFINS

The terms "gluten-free" and "wheat-free" are often confused. A person diagnosed as "coeliac" is unable to eat any foods containing gluten, including wheat, oats, barley and rye, while someone who is wheat-intolerant might be able to include the other grains in their diet. The recipes in this section are suitable for both gluten-free and wheat-free diets.

There are several gluten-free alternative flours and starches available in health food and speciality shops: brown and white rice flours, maize flour (cornmeal), cornflour (cornstarch), soya flour, chickpea (gram) flour, potato flour (potato starch), tapioca flour and more. None of these flours can produce the same texture as wheat flour. It is the gluten in wheat that gives bread its springiness and other baked goods their desirable texture. On their own, the non-wheat flours produce a dense powdery texture that practically dissolves in the mouth, leaving nothing to chew. Surprisingly, by combining several of these flours, there is a marked improvement which can be enhanced even further by adding extra egg to bind it together.

One additional ingredient produces a dramatic effect: xanthan gum. This is a natural substance, produced by a micro-organism, that has been used commercially in foods (such as salad dressings) for many years. In gluten-free baking, xanthan gum helps to bind the product together to give that special tender chewiness that makes baked goods so pleasurable to eat. If you want to transform your gluten-free baking from substandard to first-class, xanthan gum is the answer! (The cost might seem expensive at first but don't let this put you off. As only a small amount is needed, a 100 g tub will go a long way: the price per batch of muffins is minimal.) Although used extensively in the food industry, it can be hard to find. The following companies supply both xanthan gum and my recommended flours:

Innovative Solutions UK Limited
Cenargo E-Logistics, The Heston Centre, International Avenue, Hounslow TW5 9NJ
Tel: 0845 601 3151 (local rate)
E-mail: info@innovative-solutions.org.uk

Barbara's Kitchen Limited
P.O. Box 54, Pontyclun, S. Wales CF72 8WD
Tel: 0845 130 6297 (local rate)
E-mail: enquiries@barbaraskitchen.co.uk

Gourmet Gluten Free Imports Ltd
12 Singleton Gardens, Clanfield, Hants PO8 0XN
Tel: 023 92 647572
Website: www.ggfi.co.uk

Although there are several brands of pre-mixed gluten-free flours available, they are often expensive and vary greatly in palatability. You can make your own top-quality gluten-free flour for a fraction of the price.

In the early part of my gluten-free experiments, chickpea flour was quickly eliminated as having an objectionable flavour, at least in a muffin! Soya flour had an unpleasant aroma so that too was avoided. Maize meal (cornmeal), although pleasant, gave the baking a distinctive "cornbread" flavour which did not make it a good base for adding other flavourings.

Product names can be misleading. British cornflour is a starch and in fact is called cornstarch in North America; it should not be confused with maize flour or cornmeal. Likewise, in Britain potato starch may be labelled potato flour as the two names seem to be used interchangeably. In other countries that might not be the case; potato starch is the required ingredient.

As those on restricted diets are already at risk of nutritional deficiencies, I recommend including some brown rice flour in the following mix, such as 2 oz (60 g) brown rice flour plus 5 oz (140 g) white rice flour. The additional flavour from the brown flour is minimal and quite pleasant. White flour is important for a light texture.

Here, then, is my recommended mix for replacing plain flour, ounce for ounce, in muffins (and many other forms of baking too, but that is beyond the scope of this book!). This quantity makes 10 oz (280 g). Sift the mixture at least twice to distribute the xanthan evenly.

7 oz (200 g) rice flour (ideally a mix of white and brown)
2 oz (60 g) potato flour (potato starch)
1 oz (30 g) tapioca flour (not granules) or cornflour (cornstarch)
1 teaspoon (5 ml) xanthan gum

You can also make up this flour replacement in bulk by increasing each item proportionately. For example, to make a triple batch each item is multiplied by 3, thus 21 oz (600 g) rice flour, 6 oz (180 g) potato flour, 3 oz (90 g) tapioca flour or cornflour, and 3 teaspoons (15 ml) xanthan gum. This should be sifted together several times and stored in a cool, dry place.

Note: When any new food is introduced to a diet, one should be alert to the possibility of adverse reactions, especially in children.

Most of the recipes in this book can be altered to suit gluten-free and wheat-free diets. (Avoid those containing oats and bran.) Remember to increase the liquid slightly, about 2-4 Tablespoons (30-60 ml), and use two eggs instead of one. The batter needs to be quite "sloppy" as rice flour is more absorbent than wheat flour. For best results, choose recipes with a higher moisture content (i.e. with added fruit or vegetables). The two examples which follow demonstrate how to make these adjustments. Enjoy!

GLUTEN-FREE BANANA MUFFINS

Makes 11-12 standard-size

7 oz (200 g) rice flour (ideally a mix of white and brown)
2 oz (60 g) potato flour
1 oz (30 g) tapioca flour or cornflour/cornstarch
1 teaspoon (5 ml) xanthan gum
1 teaspoon (5 ml) gluten-free baking powder
1 teaspoon (5 ml) bicarbonate of soda
1/2 teaspoon (2.5 ml) salt
3 large well-ripened bananas (8-10 fl oz/240-290 ml when mashed)
4 oz (110 g) fine white granulated sugar
2 eggs, beaten with a fork
3-4 fl oz (90-120 ml) milk or water
3 fl oz (90 ml) vegetable oil or 3 oz (85 g) butter, melted
2-3 oz (60-85 g) walnuts or plain chocolate chips (optional)

Method

1 Prepare tins. Preheat oven to 375-400°F (190-200°C) for a conventional oven, Gas Mark 5-6.
2 In a large bowl, sift together at least twice: flours, xanthan gum, baking powder, bicarbonate of soda and salt. (Add chocolate if using.)
3 In another bowl, mash bananas thoroughly with a potato masher. Stir in sugar, eggs, milk/water and oil/butter.
4 Pour all of wet ingredients into dry. Stir until batter is evenly mixed and no dry flour is visible. (Add walnuts if using.)
5 Spoon into tins. Bake for 20-25 minutes, until tops are lightly browned and spring back when pressed gently.

GLUTEN-FREE APPLE SPICE MUFFINS

Makes 10-12 standard-size

7 oz (200 g) rice flour (ideally a mix of white and brown)

2 oz (60 g) potato flour

1 oz (30 g) tapioca flour or cornflour/cornstarch

1 teaspoon (5 ml) xanthan gum

3 teaspoons (15 ml) gluten-free baking powder

$^1/_2$ teaspoon (2.5 ml) salt

$1^1/_2$ teaspoons (7.5 ml) mixed spice (adjust to taste)

4 oz (110 g) fine white granulated sugar

2 eggs

6 oz (170 g) finely chopped apple (I like to use Granny Smiths, but most other types should work just as well)

6-7 fl oz (180-210 ml) milk

3 fl oz (90 ml) vegetable oil or 3 oz (85 g) butter, melted

2-3 oz (60-85 g) raisins, sultanas or chopped walnuts (optional)

Optional Topping:

3 Tablespoons (45 ml) soft brown sugar

2 oz (60 g) walnuts, chopped

Method

1 Prepare muffin tins. Preheat oven to 375-400°F (190-200°C) for a conventional oven, Gas Mark 5-6.

2 In a large bowl, sift together at least twice: flours, xanthan gum, baking powder, salt, spice and sugar.

3 In another bowl, beat eggs with a fork. Stir in chopped apple and milk, followed by oil/melted butter.

4 Pour all of wet mixture into dry. Stir until evenly combined, adding dried fruit/walnuts during the final strokes. This batter is thicker than most; apple releases juice as it cooks.

5 Spoon into tins. Sprinkle with topping. Bake about 20-25 minutes until tops are lightly browned and quite firm.

APPENDIX 2

NORTH AMERICAN MEASURES AND EQUIVALENTS

These are the approximate North American volume equivalents for weights used in this book.

Note: 1 cup = 8 fluid ounces = 240 ml.

Flour

This is only a rough guide as flours can vary considerably. Please read about flour on page 7. When measuring flour by volume, it should be sifted beforehand. It might be necessary to adjust the amount of liquid in a recipe to suit your flour if you are finding the batter too thick or thin. This balance of wet and dry ingredients is important for successful baking.

10 oz (280 g) plain flour = 2¼ cups. *Substitute 1¾ cups all-purpose flour.*

9 oz (255 g) plain flour = 2 cups. *Substitute 1½ cups all-purpose flour.*

8 oz (225 g) plain flour = 1¾ cups. *Substitute 1⅓ cups all-purpose flour.*

7 oz (200 g) plain flour = 1½ cups. *Substitute 1¼ cups all-purpose flour.*

6 oz (170 g) plain flour = 1¼ cups. *Substitute 1 cup all-purpose flour.*

5 oz (140 g) plain flour = 1 cup+2 Tbsp. *Substitute ⅞ cup all-purpose flour.*

Sugar

6 oz (170 g) sugar = ¾ cup
5 oz (140 g) sugar = ⅔ cup
4 oz (110 g) sugar = ½ cup
3 oz (85 g) sugar = ⅓ cup
2 oz (60 g) sugar = ¼ cup

Ingredient	Weight	Volume
Almonds, flaked	2 oz (60 g)	½ cup
Apple, chopped	6 oz (170 g)	¾ cup, packed
Butter/Margarine	2-3 oz (60-85 g)	¼-⅓ cup
Carrot, grated	7-12 oz (200-340 g)	1-1¾ cups
Cheese, grated	3 oz (85 g)	1 cup

Ingredient	Weight	Volume
Chocolate chips	3 oz (85 g)	½ cup
Cornmeal	6 oz (170 g)	1 cup
Courgette/zucchini	12 oz (340 g)	2 cups, grated
Dried fruit	3-6 oz (85-170 g)	½-1 cup
Nuts, chopped	2-3 oz (60-85 g)	½-¾ cup
Oats	2-3 oz (60-85 g)	⅔-1 cup
Oat bran	3½ oz (105 g)	¾ cup
Summer Fruit	5 oz (140 g)	1 cup
Wheat bran (coarse)	2½ oz (75 g)	1 cup
Wheat germ	1½ oz (45 g)	½ cup

Further Notes on Measurement

Although many British units of measurement have the same names as North American (N.A.) units, they are not all identical. In general, weights are equivalent but volumes are not. Here are two differences which may prove useful:

1 British fluid ounce (fl oz) = 28.4 ml
1 N.A. fluid ounce = 29.5 ml

1 British liquid pint = 20 fl oz = 568 ml
1 N.A. liquid pint = 16 fl oz = 472 ml

For single batch muffin-baking, you can assume:
1 fl oz = 30 ml = 2 Tablespoons

To convert fluid ounces to cups, use the following:

2 fl oz = ¼ cup
3 fl oz = ⅓ cup
4 fl oz = ½ cup
5 fl oz = just under ⅔ cup
6 fl oz = ¾ cup
7 fl oz = ¾ cup + 2 Tbsp
8 fl oz = 1 cup
9 fl oz = 1 cup + 2 Tbsp
10 fl oz = 1¼ cups